BIG RIGS

by Darlene R. Stille

Content Adviser: Professor Sherry L. Field,
Department of Social Science Education, College of Education,
The University of Georgia
Reading Adviser: Dr. Linda D. Labbo,
Department of Reading Education, College of Education,
The University of Georgia

Compass Point Books

Minneapolis, Minnesota

Compass Point Books
3722 West 50th Street, #115
Minneapolis, MN 55410

Visit Compass Point Books on the Internet at *www.compasspointbooks.com* or e-mail your request to
custserv@compasspointbooks.com

Photographs ©: Photo Network/Tom Tracy, cover, 8–9; Mark E. Gibson/Visuals Unlimited, 1; Victoria
Hurst/Tom Stack and Associates, 4–5; Archive Photos, 6–7, 18–19; Unicorn Stock Photos/Eric R. Berndt,
10–11; Thomas Kitchin/Tom Stack and Associated, 12–13; John Sohlden/Visuals Unlimited, 14–15; Jeff
Greenberg/Visuals Unlimited, 16; Unicorn Stock Photos/Paul A. Hein, 20–21; Ned Therrien/Visuals
Unlimited, 22; www.ronkimball/stock.com, 24–25; W. Perry Conway/Tom Stack and Associates, 26.

Editors: E. Russell Primm and Emily J. Dolbear
Photo Researcher: Svetlana Zhurkina
Photo Selector: Melissa Voda
Designer: Melissa Voda

Library of Congress Cataloging-in-Publication Data
Stille, Darlene R.
    Big rigs / by Darlene R. Stille.
        p. cm. — (Transportation)
    Includes bibliographical references and index.
    ISBN 0-7565-0147-4 (library binding)
        1. Tractor trailer combinations—Juvenile literature. [1. Tractor trailers. 2. Trucks.] I. Title.
    TL230.15 .S765 2001
    629.224—dc21 2001001432

Table of Contents

Driving a Big Rig ——————————— 4

Up in the Cab ——————————— 6

Driving a Semi ——————————— 8

Driving a Tank Truck ——————————— 10

Driving a Dump Truck ——————————— 12

Driving a Cement Truck ——————————— 14

Driving a Moving Van ——————————— 17

Driving a Logging Truck ——————————— 18

Giving Cars a Ride ——————————— 20

Trucks That Help Trucks ——————————— 23

Monster Trucks ——————————— 24

Really Huge Trucks ——————————— 26

Glossary ——————————— 28

Did You Know? ——————————— 29

Want to Know More? ——————————— 30

Index ——————————— 32

Driving a Big Rig

Zoom! Zoom! Listen to these big rigs going down the highway. Big trucks are called big rigs.

Big rigs squeeze down city streets and country lanes. The loads they carry are called freight or cargo.

There are many kinds of trucks. Every truck has wheels and a motor. Great big trucks have a cab and a body. The driver sits in the cab. Cargo goes in the body.

Up in the Cab

6

The cab is in the front of a big rig. The driver has to climb up steps to get into the cab. The driver sits in the cab and steers the truck. Pressing pedals makes the truck stop and go.

On long trips, the driver parks the truck and sleeps in the cab. Many trucks have a small bedroom behind the driver's seat. Sometimes there are two drivers. One drives while the other sleeps.

Driving a Semi

trailer

tractor

Most big rigs are semis. *Semi* is another word for "tractor–semitrailer truck." These big rigs have two parts.

The motor and the cab are in the tractor part. The cargo goes into the trailer part. The tractor pulls the trailer. Some tractors pull two or three trailers. Semis may have sixteen or more wheels.

Driving a Tank Truck

A tank truck is like a semi. Its tractor pulls a big tank on wheels. For example, milk trucks are tank trucks. They have shiny stainless steel tanks. They pick up milk at farms and take the milk to a dairy. Milk trucks must be very clean.

Gasoline trucks are tank trucks too. They deliver gasoline to gas stations. Tank trucks also carry oil and chemicals.

Driving a Dump Truck

It's fun to watch dump trucks in action. Dump trucks carry dirt, coal, sand, or gravel. When the body of a dump truck tips up, its load of dirt, coal, sand, or gravel dumps out. Maybe you have a toy dump truck that works like this.

Driving a Cement Truck

Cement trucks mix cement while they are on their way from place to place.

A cement truck has a big barrel on the back. As the truck goes down the road, the barrel goes round and round. Blades inside the barrel mix cement. After the truck stops, workers pour cement out of the barrel.

Driving a Moving Van

Did your family ever move to another apartment or house? Maybe you used a moving van. Vans are one-piece trucks.

You can use a van to move across town. You can use a van to move to a faraway city too. Other vans deliver things you buy in a store. They deliver clothes washers and dryers and all kinds of furniture.

Driving a Logging Truck

Logging trucks are flatbed trucks. Flatbed trucks have no sides.

Logging trucks carry big logs. The logs have been cut from trees in a forest. A crane lifts the logs onto the flatbed truck. Chains keep the logs from rolling off.

Giving Cars a Ride

How can a car go down a road without touching the ground? It can ride on a big rig made for carrying cars!

These big rigs are called auto transporters. They deliver cars to auto dealers. Auto transporters have special racks that hold the cars steady. Some transporters can even carry boats.

Trucks That Help Trucks

Snowplows keep roads open after a snowstorm. These trucks have big blades that push snow off the road. They also spread salt or sand on the road to make it less slippery. Roads are safer for trucks and cars after the snowplow goes through.

Big tow trucks help trucks that break down. They tow the trucks to a garage where trucks are fixed.

Monster Trucks

Monster trucks do not carry cargo. Monster trucks are for fun.

Most monster trucks are pickup trucks with huge tires. The huge tires allow monster trucks to jump over rows of cars. Monster trucks also race one another. Some people go to stadiums to watch monster trucks for fun.

Really Huge Trucks

Some trucks are so big that they cannot drive on the highway. The biggest off-highway trucks weigh about 500,000 pounds (227,000 kilograms). That is more than forty elephants weigh!

Most of these huge trucks are dump trucks. Some are used in mines and rock quarries.

On or off the highway, trucks are important. Your clothes, your food, and everything you use came from somewhere on a truck.

Glossary

cargo—goods carried by ship, plane, or truck

crane—a machine with a long arm used to lift and move heavy objects

freight—cargo carried from place to place

monster—huge

quarries—places where stone is dug from the ground

stainless steel—steel that does not rust or tarnish

trailer—a vehicle that is towed by a car or truck and is used to carry things

Did You Know?

Long-distance truck drivers travel 550 to 600 miles (885 to 966 kilometers) per day.

The first long-distance trip by a truck carrying freight was made in 1911. The truck was called the Pioneer Freighter. It weighed 7 tons when loaded with goods. The trip from Denver to Los Angeles took sixty-six days!

The bulldog on the front of Mack trucks was created by Mack employee Alfred Fellow Masury. He created it while recovering from surgery.

Want to Know More?

At the Library

Malam, John, and Mike Foster (illustrator). *Big Rigs.* New York: Simon and Schuster, 1998.

Marston, Hope Irvin. *Big Rigs.* New York: Cobblehill, 1993.

Schleifer, Jay. *Big Rigs.* Mankato: Minn.: Capstone Press, 1996.

On the Web

Virtual Truck World

http://truck.chat.ru/PAGES/ustruck.html

For pictures and descriptions of many big rigs

Mack Trucks History

http://www.macktrucks.com/history/hist_frm.htm

For information on the history of Mack trucks

Through the Mail

The American Trucking Association

2200 Mill Road

Alexandria, VA 22314

On the Road

The Pacific Northwest Truck Museum

PO Box 875

Wilsonville, OR 97070

503/694–5109

For information and exhibits on many kinds of trucks, including big rigs

Index

auto transporters, 21

big rigs, 5, 7, 9

cabs, 5, 7, 9

cargo. *See freight.*

cement trucks, 15

drivers, 7

dump trucks, 13, 27

flatbed trucks, 19

freight, 5, 9

gasoline trucks, 11

logging trucks, 19

milk trucks, 11

monster trucks, 25

motors, 5, 9

moving vans, 17

off-highway trucks, 27

pickup trucks, 25

semis, 9

snowplows, 23

tank trucks, 11

tow trucks, 23

trailers, 9

vans, 17

wheels, 5, 9

About the Author

Darlene R. Stille is a science editor and writer. She has lived in Chicago, Illinois, all her life. When she was in high school, she fell in love with science. While attending the University of Illinois, she discovered that she also enjoyed writing. Today she feels fortunate to have a career that allows her to pursue both her interests. Darlene R. Stille has written more than thirty books for young people.